Encryption Demystified

The Key to Securing Your Digital Life

Preface

In our digital age, the protection of sensitive information is becoming increasingly important. Every day, we rely on encryption to keep our personal and financial information secure while we browse the web, use mobile devices, or communicate with others. Encryption is a powerful tool that can provide strong security, but it is not always easy to understand.

This book aims to demystify encryption and make it accessible to a wide audience. We have created a comprehensive guide to encryption that covers the main concepts, techniques, and standards used in modern encryption systems. The book is intended for anyone who is interested in encryption, from beginners to experts, and from technology enthusiasts to business professionals.

We start with an overview of encryption and its applications, followed by an explanation of the different types of encryption techniques, including symmetric key encryption, public key encryption, and hybrid encryption. We also delve into the technical details of key generation, management, and distribution, and explore the challenges of implementing encryption in practice.

Throughout the book, we use real-life examples, exercises and scenarios to illustrate the concepts and techniques, and we provide practical advice on how to choose the right encryption system for different situations. We also discuss the legal and regulatory frameworks that govern encryption, including the European Union General Data Protection Regulation

(GDPR), the Payment Card Industry Data Security Standard (PCI DSS), and other industry-specific standards.

We hope that this book will provide you with a solid foundation in encryption and empower you to use encryption to protect your data and privacy. We welcome feedback and suggestions, and we hope that you find this book informative and engaging.

But still a point of attention. Developments in this area are moving at lightning speed. It is therefore not inconceivable that some information will quickly become outdated. It is important that you, as the reader, are aware of this and do further research for your own specific situation.

Happy reading!

A. Scholtens

Table of Contents

Chapter 1: Introduction to Encryption

Encryption is the practice of converting information into a code to prevent unauthorized access and maintain the privacy and security of data. In this chapter, we will discuss the definition and history of encryption, as well as its significance in today's world.

1.1 Definition of Encryption

Encryption can be defined as the process of transforming information into a code to prevent unauthorized access. This code, known as ciphertext, can only be deciphered by those who have the proper key. The key is used to encrypt and decrypt the data, converting the ciphertext back into its original form, called plaintext.

Examples of Ciphertext:

1. Substitution Cipher: In this type of cipher, each letter of the plaintext is replaced with another letter or symbol to form the ciphertext. For example, consider the following plaintext message: "HELLO". Using a substitution cipher, the ciphertext message could be "UHYYB".

2. Transposition Cipher: In this type of cipher, the letters of the plaintext message are rearranged to form the ciphertext. For example, consider the following plaintext message: "HELLO". Using a transposition cipher, the ciphertext message could be "LELOH".

3. Block Cipher: In this type of cipher, the plaintext message is divided into blocks of a fixed size, and each block is then encrypted to form

the ciphertext. For example, consider the following plaintext message: "HELLO". If the block size is two, the first two letters "HE" would form the first block, and the next two letters "LL" would form the second block. The ciphertext message would be the encrypted blocks.

Encryption is used to protect sensitive information such as financial data, medical records, personal information, and confidential business information. It is also used in secure communication, such as email and instant messaging, to ensure that the information transmitted over the internet is protected from prying eyes.

1.2 History of Encryption

Encryption has been used since ancient times to protect secret messages. The earliest known use of encryption dates back to the Greeks, who used simple substitution ciphers to encode messages. In the Middle Ages, more complex encryption methods were developed, including the use of polyalphabetic ciphers.

During World War II, encryption became a critical tool for military communication. The Germans used the Enigma machine to encrypt their messages, while the Allies used the famous Colossus computer to crack the code. The development of computers in the 20th century brought about a new era of encryption, making it possible to encrypt large amounts of data quickly and securely.

Today, encryption is a critical component of cybersecurity, protecting sensitive information from cyber threats such as hackers, viruses, and malware. With the increasing reliance on technology and the internet, encryption is more important than ever in protecting personal and business information.

Examples of Encryption in Today's World

1. Secure Online Banking: When you log into your online banking account, your financial information is encrypted to prevent unauthorized access. This means that even if a hacker intercepts the information as it is transmitted over the internet, they will not be able to read it.

2. Protecting Health Information: In the healthcare industry, encryption is used to protect sensitive patient information, such as medical records and personal information. This helps to maintain the privacy and security of the patient's information and ensures that it is only accessible by authorized individuals.

3. Encrypted Communication: Encryption is used in communication tools such as email and instant messaging to ensure that the information transmitted between users is protected from prying eyes. For example, popular instant messaging apps such as WhatsApp and Signal use end-to-end encryption to ensure that the messages sent between users are secure.

4. Protecting Data in the Cloud: Encryption is also used to protect data stored in the cloud. This means that even if a hacker gains access to the data, they will not be able to read it without the proper key.

Encryption is a critical component of modern-day cybersecurity, helping to protect sensitive information from unauthorized access. From ancient times to the present day, encryption has evolved to meet the changing needs of society and technology. As we become increasingly reliant on technology, encryption will continue to play a vital role in protecting our personal and business information.

Exercises Chapter 1 The Ciphertext

1. Decryption of Substitution Cipher: Given the following ciphertext message "UHYYB", decode it to the original plaintext message.

2. Decryption of Block Cipher: Given the following ciphertext message "HG EL LO", decode it to the original plaintext message.

3. Decryption of Vigenère Cipher Given the following ciphertext message: "ROLW EKAD YVEE VGTX", decode it to the original plaintext message.

Note: These exercises are meant to be simple and introductory in nature. In real-world scenarios, encryption and decryption of ciphertext is much more complex and secure, involving the use of complex algorithms and keys to prevent unauthorized access.

Chapter 2: Encryption Types

The primary purpose of encryption is to protect sensitive information from unauthorized access. There are several different types of encryption, each with its own strengths and weaknesses. In this chapter, we will explore the four main types of encryption: symmetric encryption, asymmetric encryption, stream encryption, and block encryption.

2.1 Symmetric Encryption

Introduction: Symmetric encryption is a method of encryption where the same key is used to both encrypt and decrypt the data. It is one of the most commonly used encryption techniques due to its simplicity and efficiency.

2.1.1 Algorithms: AES (Advanced Encryption Standard)

The Advanced Encryption Standard (AES) is a symmetric encryption algorithm that was first adopted by the U.S. government in 2001 and has since become the most widely used encryption algorithm in the world. AES uses a fixed block size of 128 bits and can support key lengths of 128, 192, and 256 bits.

AES is a substitution-permutation network (SPN) encryption algorithm, which means it uses substitution and permutation to encrypt data. In a substitution operation, the algorithm replaces plaintext characters with ciphertext characters, while in a permutation operation, the algorithm rearranges the order of the characters. The combination of these two operations provides a high level of security, making AES very difficult to crack.

AES is considered to be a highly secure algorithm because it has been thoroughly analyzed and tested by cryptologists, security experts, and the National Institute of Standards and Technology (NIST). It has been subjected to extensive cryptanalysis and has passed multiple security evaluations, making it one of the most trusted encryption algorithms available.

AES is used in a variety of applications, including secure communication, data storage, and secure payment systems. It is also commonly used to encrypt sensitive information in government and military communications, as well as in financial institutions and other organizations that handle sensitive data.

Overall, AES is a highly efficient and secure symmetric encryption algorithm that provides a high level of protection for sensitive information. Whether you are an individual looking to secure your personal data or an organization looking to protect sensitive information, AES is a reliable and trusted encryption solution.

2.1.2 DES (Data Encryption Standard)

The Data Encryption Standard (DES) is a symmetric encryption algorithm that was first developed in the 1970s and was widely used in the following decades. DES was initially developed by IBM and was later standardized by the National Institute of Standards and Technology (NIST) in 1977.

DES uses a fixed block size of 64 bits and a key length of 56 bits. The algorithm works by dividing the plaintext into 64-bit blocks and then encrypting each block using the same key. The key is used to determine the encryption algorithm's substitution and permutation operations, which transform the plaintext into ciphertext.

DES was considered to be a highly secure encryption algorithm when it was first introduced. However, with the advent of faster computers and advances in cryptography, DES has been found to be vulnerable to certain attacks and is no longer considered secure for sensitive data.

Despite its weaknesses, DES is still widely used in some applications, particularly in legacy systems where it may not be practical to upgrade to a more secure encryption algorithm. DES is also used in certain financial applications, where its use is mandated by regulations, and in some low-security applications, where the encryption requirements are not as stringent.

While DES has been replaced by AES as the standard symmetric encryption algorithm, it still has a place in certain applications and continues to be widely used. However, it is important to consider the security implications of using DES and to upgrade to a more secure encryption algorithm if necessary.

2.1.3 3DES (Triple DES)

Triple DES (3DES) is an extension of the Data Encryption Standard (DES) algorithm and is a symmetric encryption method. As its name suggests, 3DES applies the DES encryption algorithm three times to the data, using three different keys.

The basic idea behind 3DES is to increase the security of DES by using three encryption keys and three encryption rounds, making it more difficult for an attacker to break the encryption. In 3DES, the plaintext is encrypted using the first key, decrypted using the second key, and then encrypted again using the third key.

3DES uses a key length of 112 bits or 168 bits, which is much longer than the 56-bit key length used in DES. The increased key length makes it much more difficult for an attacker to brute-force the encryption, as they would need to try all possible combinations of the key, which is a very time-consuming process.

3DES is widely used in applications where a higher level of security is required, such as in financial transactions and data storage. However, despite its increased security, 3DES has been found to be vulnerable to certain attacks, particularly in the context of cryptographic attacks that take advantage of weaknesses in the encryption algorithm.

3DES is a more secure alternative to the original DES algorithm, but its use is becoming increasingly rare as it has been largely replaced by Advanced Encryption Standard (AES) in many applications. However, it is still widely used in legacy systems and in certain applications where the increased security provided by 3DES is necessary.

2.2 Key Generation, Management, and Distribution

Key Generation, Management, and Distribution is an important aspect of symmetric encryption. In symmetric encryption, the same key is used for both encryption and decryption, making it critical to ensure the secure generation, management, and distribution of the key.

Key generation refers to the process of creating a secure key for the encryption and decryption of data. The key must be random and unique to ensure the security of the encryption. The key can be generated using various methods, such as random number generators, or by using a password-based key derivation function.

Key management refers to the process of storing, managing, and protecting the key. The key must be stored securely and must be protected from unauthorized access. This can be done by storing the key in a secure location, such as a secure server or encrypted storage device, and by controlling access to the key through authentication and authorization mechanisms.

Key distribution refers to the process of sharing the key between the sender and the receiver. In symmetric encryption, the same key is used for both encryption and decryption, making it critical to ensure that the key is securely shared between the sender and the receiver. This can be done through various methods, such as manual key exchange or by using a secure key exchange protocol.

Key generation, management, and distribution is a crucial aspect of symmetric encryption. The security of the encryption relies on the secure generation, management, and distribution of the key, making it critical to ensure the protection of the key from unauthorized access. If the key is compromised, the security of the encryption is at risk, making it important to implement secure key generation, management, and distribution practices to ensure the security of the encryption.

2.3 Strengths and Weaknesses

One of the main strengths of symmetric encryption is its speed and efficiency. It is much faster than asymmetric encryption and can encrypt and decrypt large amounts of data in a short amount of time. Another advantage is that it is relatively simple to implement and does not require a lot of computational resources.

One of the main weaknesses of symmetric encryption is the key distribution problem. Since the same key is used for both encryption and decryption, it must be securely shared between the sender and receiver. This can be a challenge, especially when communicating with multiple parties. Additionally, if the key is lost or stolen, the encrypted data cannot be decrypted, making symmetric encryption vulnerable to key theft.

Example: Suppose that Alice wants to send an email to Bob containing sensitive information. To ensure the confidentiality of the information, she decides to use symmetric encryption.

She chooses the AES algorithm and generates a secret key. She then uses the AES algorithm and the secret key to encrypt the email and send it to Bob.

When Bob receives the email, he uses the same AES algorithm and the same secret key to decrypt the message. Since the same key is used for both encryption and decryption, the information remains confidential and secure.

In this example, symmetric encryption was used to secure the confidentiality of sensitive information while communicating over the internet. By using the AES algorithm and a secret key, Alice and Bob were able to ensure the confidentiality of their communications.

Symmetric encryption is a widely used encryption technique that provides fast and efficient encryption and decryption. It is an important tool for securing confidential information and protecting against unauthorized access. However, it also has its weaknesses, including the key distribution problem, which must be carefully managed to ensure the security of the encrypted data.

Exercises Chapter 2 Encryption Types

1. What are the key sizes supported by AES?

2. What are the steps involved in the AES encryption process?

3. What is the difference between AES-128 and AES-256?

4. What is the block size of the DES algorithm?

5. How many rounds does the DES algorithm use for encryption?

6. Suppose you have a plaintext message "HELLO" that you want to encrypt using the DES algorithm. What will be the size of the ciphertext output?

7. What is the key size for 3DES? How does it compare to the key size for DES?

8. In what mode of operation can 3DES be used to encrypt messages that are larger than one block?

9. Suppose you are given a plaintext message "HELLO" (in ASCII), a 3DES key of "ABCDEF1234567890", and a ciphertext of "81B4F7C063E115EE". Decrypt the ciphertext to recover the original message.

10. In symmetric encryption, the same key is used for:

    a) Encryption only
    b) Decryption only
    c) Both encryption and decryption

11. Key management refers to the process of:

a) Creating a secure key for encryption

b) Storing, managing, and protecting the key

c) Sharing the key between the sender and receiver

12. One of the main weaknesses of symmetric encryption is:

a) Its speed and efficiency

b) Its simplicity to implement

c) The key distribution problem

Chapter 3 Asymmetric Encryption

Introduction: Asymmetric encryption, also known as public-key cryptography, is a type of encryption that uses two different keys for encryption and decryption. Unlike symmetric encryption, where the same key is used for both encryption and decryption, asymmetric encryption uses one key for encryption and another key for decryption. This makes it a more secure method of encryption compared to symmetric encryption, as the keys can be generated, managed, and distributed securely, ensuring the protection of sensitive information.

3.1 Algorithms

There are several asymmetric encryption algorithms in use today, but the most commonly used algorithms include RSA, ECC, and Diffie-Hellman.

1. **RSA (Rivest-Shamir-Adleman)**

   RSA is a widely used asymmetric encryption algorithm that is known for its security and efficiency. It is used in various applications, including SSL/TLS certificates, digital signatures, and secure email.

   RSA works by using two keys: a public key and a private key. The public key is used to encrypt messages and the private key is used to decrypt messages. When a message is encrypted with the recipient's public key, only the private key of the recipient can be used to decrypt it. This makes RSA a secure method for transmitting sensitive information, as the private key never leaves the recipient's possession.

RSA uses the mathematical properties of large prime numbers to encrypt and decrypt messages. The security of RSA is based on the difficulty of factoring large prime numbers, which makes it computationally infeasible to determine the private key from the public key. This makes RSA a strong algorithm for protecting sensitive information, such as credit card numbers, passwords, and personal identification numbers (PINs).

One of the main benefits of RSA is that it can be used for both encryption and digital signatures. A digital signature is a way to prove the authenticity and integrity of a message, and RSA can be used to generate and verify digital signatures. This makes RSA a versatile algorithm that can be used in a wide range of applications that require secure communication.

2. ECC (Elliptic Curve Cryptography)

ECC is a relatively new asymmetric encryption algorithm that is known for its efficiency and security. It is commonly used in mobile devices, smart cards, and other security-sensitive applications where resource constraints are a concern.

Elliptic Curve Cryptography (ECC) is a modern asymmetric encryption algorithm that is gaining popularity due to its efficiency and security. Unlike RSA, which uses large prime numbers to generate keys, ECC uses the mathematics of elliptic curves to generate keys. This makes ECC a more secure algorithm, as it requires much shorter keys than RSA to provide the same level of security.

ECC is commonly used in mobile devices, smart cards, and other security-sensitive applications where resource constraints are a concern. It provides the same level of security as RSA, but requires significantly less computational resources, making it a more attractive option for devices with limited resources, such as smartphones and smart cards.

Additionally, ECC is becoming increasingly popular for securing internet transactions, such as online banking and e-commerce transactions, as well as for encrypting sensitive data, such as personal information, and communication between parties. This makes ECC an important aspect of modern cryptography and a valuable tool for protecting sensitive information in today's digital age.

3. Diffie-Hellman

Diffie-Hellman is an asymmetric encryption algorithm that is used for secure key exchange. It is used to securely exchange keys between two parties without having to transmit the key over the network.

Diffie-Hellman is a fundamental concept in cryptography that was first published in 1976. It is used to securely exchange cryptographic keys between two parties, typically in a communication network. The algorithm is based on the idea of using public and private keys to establish a secure key exchange.

The basic idea behind Diffie-Hellman is that two parties, Alice and Bob, can agree on a shared secret key without ever transmitting the key over the network. They start by each choosing their own private keys, which are kept secret. They then use these private keys to generate public keys, which are shared with each other. Using these public keys, they can then generate a shared secret key.

This shared secret key can then be used for secure communication between Alice and Bob. Because the private keys are kept secret, even if an eavesdropper is able to intercept the public keys, they will not be able to determine the shared secret key.

Diffie-Hellman is widely used in secure communication protocols, including SSL/TLS, IPSec, and SSH. It is also used in various applications, such as secure email, virtual private networks (VPNs), and file transfers.

Diffie-Hellman is an essential algorithm in cryptography that provides a secure way to exchange keys between two parties. Its popularity and widespread use make it a critical component of secure communication networks.

Example:

Alice and Bob want to establish a shared secret key using Diffie-Hellman. Alice chooses a prime number $p = 23$ and a base $g = 5$. Alice's secret key is $a = 6$, and Bob's secret key is $b = 15$. What is the shared secret key?

Answer:

In the given example, Alice and Bob have agreed on a public prime number **p** and a generator **g** modulo **p**. Alice has a secret exponent **a** and Bob has a secret exponent **b**. They each use their secret exponents to calculate their public keys, **A** and **B**, respectively.

Using these values, Alice calculates the shared secret key **s** by taking Bob's public key **B** and raising it to her secret exponent **a**, modulo **p**. Bob can calculate the same shared secret key by taking Alice's public key **A** and raising it to his secret exponent **b**, modulo **p**. The resulting shared secret key **s** is the same for both Alice and Bob, and can be used for symmetric encryption.

In the given example, Alice's public key is **A = g^a mod p = 5^6 mod 23 = 8**, and Bob's public key is **B = g^b mod p = 5^15 mod 23 = 19**. To calculate the shared secret key **s**, Alice takes Bob's public key **B** and raises it to her secret exponent **a** modulo **p**: **s = B^a mod p = 19^6 mod 23 = 2**. Similarly, Bob can calculate the same shared secret key by taking Alice's public key **A** and raising it to his secret exponent **b** modulo **p**: **s = A^b mod p = 8^15 mod 23 = 2**. Thus, both Alice and Bob have arrived at the same shared secret key **s = 2**.

3.2 Key Generation, Management, and Distribution:

Key generation, management, and distribution are essential elements of asymmetric encryption. The keys used in asymmetric encryption consist of a public key and a private key, and both keys must be generated, managed, and distributed securely.

The public key is used for encryption, while the private key is used for decryption. The keys are typically generated by a trusted third party, known as a certificate authority (CA), who then signs and issues digital certificates that contain the public key. The digital certificates can be used to verify the identity of the owner of the public key and ensure that the key has not been altered.

The public key can be freely shared and distributed, as it is used for encryption. However, the private key must be kept confidential and protected, as it is used for decryption and must not be disclosed to anyone other than the owner.

The management of the keys is critical, as the security of the encryption relies on the protection of the keys. Key management should include regular updates, backup, and secure storage of the keys. In addition, key distribution should be done in a secure manner, typically through secure communication channels, such as encrypted email or secure file transfer.

The success of asymmetric encryption relies on the secure generation, management, and distribution of the keys. Ensuring that these components are in place will help to protect sensitive information from unauthorized access and ensure the privacy of communications.

3.3 Public Key Infrastructure (PKI):

Public Key Infrastructure (PKI) is a system for managing and distributing digital certificates that are used to secure communications, transactions, and applications. PKI is the foundation for secure asymmetric encryption and provides the necessary infrastructure for secure key generation, management, and distribution.

In PKI, digital certificates are issued by a trusted third party, known as a certificate authority (CA), who verifies the identity of the parties involved in a transaction. The digital certificates contain the public key of a party and are used to encrypt messages or perform digital signatures. The private key is kept secret by the owner and is used to decrypt messages or to sign digital messages.

PKI provides the necessary infrastructure for secure key generation, management, and distribution, including certificate revocation lists, certificate policies, and secure certificate distribution channels. PKI ensures the authenticity and integrity of digital certificates, allowing organizations to trust the authenticity of the parties involved in a transaction.

PKI is widely used in secure communications and transactions, including SSL/TLS, digital signatures, and secure email. It provides a secure and reliable means of exchanging and protecting sensitive information, making it an essential component of secure asymmetric encryption.

3.4 Digital Signatures and Certificates

Digital signatures and certificates play an important role in asymmetric encryption by providing a secure way to verify the identity of a party and ensure the authenticity of the data. A digital signature is created by encrypting a hash of the data with the private key, while a digital certificate is an electronic document that contains the public key and is issued and signed by a certificate authority (CA).

Asymmetric encryption is a secure and efficient method of encryption that provides the infrastructure for secure communication over the internet. With the growing demand for secure communication, asymmetric encryption is becoming increasingly important, as it provides a secure way to exchange sensitive information without having to worry about the keys being intercepted or stolen. Whether it's for secure communication, digital signatures, or secure key exchange, asymmetric encryption is an essential tool for protecting sensitive information in today's digital world.

Exercises Chapter 3 Asymmetric Encryption

1. Generate an RSA key pair with a modulus of 187 and public exponent of 5. What is the private exponent?
2. Encrypt the message "HELLO" using the RSA public key (3233, 17), where 3233 is the modulus and 17 is the public exponent. Convert the message to a number using ASCII encoding.

3. Decrypt the ciphertext 1233 using the RSA private key (3233, 413), where 3233 is the modulus and 413 is the private exponent. What is the original message?

4. What is the key advantage of using Elliptic Curve Cryptography (ECC) compared to other public key cryptography systems like RSA?

5. What is a point on an elliptic curve?

6. How is a public key generated in ECC?

7. A company wants to set up a Public Key Infrastructure (PKI) for their employees to use for secure email communication. They want to use a hierarchical model with a root CA and multiple subordinate CAs. They plan to issue two types of certificates: one for email encryption and another for email signing.

   i. What is a root CA in a PKI, and what is its role?

      a. The root CA is the first CA in the hierarchy, and its role is to issue and sign the subordinate CA's certificate.

      b. The root CA is the CA that signs end-entity certificates, and its role is to verify the certificate holder's identity.

      c. The root CA is the CA that manages revocation of certificates, and its role is to ensure that revoked certificates cannot be used.

ii.   What is the purpose of a subordinate CA in a PKI?

    a. To issue and sign end-entity certificates

    b. To manage the revocation of certificates

    c. To issue and sign the root CA's certificate

iii. What is the difference between an email encryption certificate and an email signing certificate?

    a. An email encryption certificate and an email signing certificate have the same purpose.

    b. An email encryption certificate is used to sign email messages, while an email signing certificate is used to encrypt email messages.

    c. An email encryption certificate is used to encrypt email messages, while an email signing certificate is used to sign email messages.

Chapter 4: Stream and Block Encryption

Introduction: Encryption is an essential aspect of computer security, and there are two primary forms of encryption: stream encryption and block encryption. Both forms of encryption serve to protect sensitive data from unauthorized access and modification. The choice between stream and block encryption depends on the specific requirements of the data being protected.

4.1 Stream Encryption

Stream encryption is a type of encryption that encrypts data in real-time as it is being transmitted or stored. It uses a small amount of encryption data to encrypt a large amount of plaintext. The data is encrypted one byte at a time, making it highly efficient and ideal for use with real-time data such as audio, video, and voice.

4.1.1 Algorithms

1. RC4 is a stream encryption algorithm that is widely used for its speed and efficiency. It was developed by Ron Rivest in 1987 and was once considered to be one of the strongest encryption algorithms. However, several security vulnerabilities have been discovered over the years, making it less secure than other encryption algorithms. Despite its weaknesses, RC4 is still widely used in a variety of applications, including SSL/TLS, WEP, and WPA.

SSL/TLS (Secure Socket Layer/Transport Layer Security): SSL/TLS is a security protocol used to encrypt communications over the internet. It is used to secure sensitive information, such as credit card numbers, login credentials, and other sensitive data, as it travels over the internet. It provides end-to-end encryption and ensures the authenticity of the communicating parties.

WEP (Wired Equivalent Privacy): WEP was the first widely used security protocol for wireless local area networks (WLANs). It is a symmetric encryption algorithm that uses a shared key for encryption and decryption. WEP has been widely criticized for its poor security, and it has been replaced by more secure protocols, such as WPA and WPA2.

WPA (Wi-Fi Protected Access): WPA is a security protocol used to secure wireless local area networks (WLANs). It is an improvement over WEP and provides stronger security by using a combination of encryption algorithms, such as TKIP (Temporal Key Integrity Protocol) and AES (Advanced Encryption Standard). WPA2, which is the latest version of WPA, provides even stronger security by using the AES encryption algorithm.

The algorithm works by using a key to encrypt plaintext and produce ciphertext, which can then be decrypted using the same key. The algorithm generates a stream of pseudo-random numbers, which are then used to XOR the plaintext, resulting in the ciphertext. The algorithm is considered to be very fast and efficient, making it ideal for use in situations where speed is a concern.

2. Blowfish:

Blowfish is a symmetric encryption algorithm that uses a key to encrypt and decrypt data. It was designed to be fast and secure, with a focus on efficiency and ease of implementation. Unlike other encryption algorithms that use large blocks of data, blowfish operates on small, 64-bit blocks, which makes it suitable for use in applications that require high-speed encryption.

The algorithm uses a key-dependent substitution and permutation (S-box) mechanism to encrypt the data. This mechanism works by taking plaintext and transforming it into ciphertext using a combination of substitution and permutation operations, which are controlled by the key.

Blowfish can be used with different modes of operation, which determine how the plaintext is encrypted and how the ciphertext is decrypted. The most commonly used modes of operation are Electronic Codebook (ECB), Cipher Block Chaining (CBC), and Output Feedback (OFB).

In ECB mode, the plaintext is divided into blocks, and each block is encrypted independently of the others. This makes ECB mode vulnerable to patterns in the plaintext and can lead to repeated ciphertext blocks, making it easier to decrypt the message.

In CBC mode, each block of plaintext is XORed with the previous ciphertext block before it is encrypted, making it more secure than ECB mode.

In OFB mode, the encryption process is decoupled from the encryption key, and a separate stream of pseudorandom bits is generated and encrypted, which is then XORed with the plaintext to produce the ciphertext.

Each mode of operation has its own strengths and weaknesses, and the choice of mode will depend on the specific requirements of the application

Due to its speed and security, blowfish is widely used in various applications, such as virtual private networks (VPNs), firewalls, and disk encryption.

4.2 Block Encryption

Block encryption is a type of encryption that encrypts data in fixed-size blocks. It encrypts data in larger chunks, making it more secure than stream encryption. Block encryption is typically used to encrypt files, email messages, and other data that can be stored and transmitted in blocks.

4.2.1 Algorithms

1. XTS (XEX-based Tweaked CodeBook mode with ciphertext stealing):

   XTS is a mode of operation for block ciphers that is specifically designed for disk encryption. It uses a block cipher algorithm, such as AES, to encrypt data in a specific manner to ensure secure encryption of disk-based data storage. XTS provides high security by using a combination of a key-dependent substitution and permutation mechanism, as well as a tweak value that is derived from the block index, to encrypt the data.

The algorithm operates on data blocks of a fixed size, usually 128 bits, and encrypts each block independently. The tweak value is combined with the encryption key to produce a unique key for each data block. This helps to prevent related-key attacks, which can compromise the security of the encryption.

XTS is widely used in full disk encryption and encrypted file systems because of its high security and efficiency. It is also used in various applications where data confidentiality and integrity are a concern, such as in the storage of sensitive information.

4.2.2 Modes of Operation:
1. ECB (Electronic Codebook):

ECB, or Electronic Codebook, is a mode of operation used for block encryption algorithms. It works by dividing the plaintext into fixed-sized blocks and then encrypting each block independently. This means that if two identical blocks of plaintext are encrypted using ECB, the resulting ciphertext blocks will be identical.

This simplicity of ECB makes it easy to implement, but it also makes it vulnerable to security attacks, such as repeated plaintext attacks. In this type of attack, an attacker can identify patterns in the encrypted data by observing the encrypted blocks of data that correspond to the same plaintext blocks. As a result, ECB is generally not recommended for use in secure applications.

2. CBC (Cipher Block Chaining):

Cipher Block Chaining (CBC) is a widely used encryption mode in block encryption algorithms. Unlike the Electronic Codebook (ECB) mode, which encrypts each block of data independently, CBC uses the ciphertext of the previous block to encrypt the current block. This means that the encryption of one block is dependent on the encryption of the previous block, making it a more secure mode of encryption.

In CBC mode, an Initialization Vector (IV) is used as the first block of ciphertext. The IV is a random value that is generated and used to encrypt the first block of data. The IV is then combined with the encrypted block to encrypt the next block, and this process continues until all the data is encrypted. This creates a chain of encrypted blocks, which makes the encryption more secure because the same plaintext block will encrypt to a different ciphertext block each time.

Today, CBC is commonly used in various applications that require secure data transmission and storage, such as SSL/TLS protocols, file systems encryption, and encrypted databases. The use of CBC mode, in conjunction with a strong encryption algorithm, makes the encryption more secure and resistant to attacks.

3. OFB (Output Feedback):

OFB is a mode of operation used in block encryption algorithms to generate a secure and unique key stream that can be used to encrypt the data. The key stream is generated based on the encryption key and an initialization vector (IV). In OFB, the encryption of each block of data is dependent on the key stream generated for that block, and not on any previous blocks of data. This makes OFB a suitable choice for encryption in scenarios where data needs to be transmitted in real-time, such as in a streaming video or audio transmission.

However, OFB has some limitations, such as the requirement for a secure method for transmitting the IV and the vulnerability to errors in the encrypted data stream. Despite these limitations, OFB is still widely used in various encryption applications, including secure communication protocols, disk encryption, and encrypted file systems.

4. CFB (Cipher Feedback):

CFB (Cipher Feedback) is a mode of operation for block encryption algorithms, such as AES or DES. Unlike ECB or CBC, which encrypts each block of data independently, CFB operates by using the ciphertext of the previous block to encrypt the current block. In CFB, the plaintext is XORed with a keystream generated from the encryption algorithm, rather than being encrypted directly. The keystream is generated based on the encryption key and an initialization vector (IV), and it is used to encrypt the data block-by-block.

CFB provides the confidentiality of data, meaning that the encrypted data can only be decrypted by someone who has the encryption key. The mode of operation also provides a level of integrity, as any changes to the ciphertext will result in different decrypted data. However, CFB has some limitations when compared to other modes of operation, such as CBC. For example, CFB does not provide message authentication, which means that an attacker could potentially manipulate the ciphertext without detection.

CFB is commonly used in applications where confidentiality and a high degree of encryption are required, such as secure communications or disk encryption. Despite its limitations, CFB remains an important mode of operation in modern cryptography and continues to be used in various applications today.

4.3 Padding and Initialization Vectors (IVs):

Padding is used to make sure that messages have the correct size for encryption. If the message to be encrypted is not long enough to fill an entire block, padding is added to the end of the message to fill the block. The padding is added in such a way that it does not affect the original message but ensures that the encryption process can be performed correctly. This is important because many encryption algorithms, such as block encryption algorithms, require that messages be a certain size.

Initialization Vectors (IVs) play a critical role in ensuring the security of encrypted messages. An IV is a random value that is used to initialize the encryption process. It is combined with the encryption key to produce the initial state of the encryption process, which is then used to encrypt the message. This ensures that even if the same encryption key and message are used, the resulting ciphertext will be different each time, as the IV will be different. This provides an added layer of security to the encryption process, as an attacker would have to know the specific IV used in order to decrypt the message.

Examples:

Today, encryption is used in many different areas of our lives, from online banking and shopping to secure communication through messaging and email. For example, SSL/TLS certificates use stream encryption to secure the transmission of sensitive data between web browsers and servers. Disk encryption, such as BitLocker in Windows, uses block encryption to protect data stored on a disk. In addition, encryption is also used in secure communication apps like WhatsApp and Signal, where end-to-end encryption is used to protect messages from being intercepted and read by unauthorized parties.

Exercises Chapter 4 Stream and Block Encryption

1. Alice wants to encrypt the message "HELLO" using a stream cipher that generates a keystream of "01101". What is the resulting ciphertext?

2. Bob is using the RC4 stream cipher to encrypt a message using a secret key of "10101100 11100011 00011100 00101011". The plaintext is "SECRET MESSAGE", which can be converted to binary as "01010011 01000101 01000011 01010010 01000101 01010100 00100000 01001101 01000101 01010011 01010011 01000001 01000111 01000101". What is the resulting ciphertext?

3. Eve is trying to crack the stream cipher that Alice and Bob are using. She knows that the plaintext message is "TOP SECRET", and that the keystream is "10010". She intercepts the ciphertext as "00011110 10001010 01000000 00011000 00011111 10001010 01001000". Can she recover the plaintext message?

4. Using the Data Encryption Standard (DES), encrypt the message "HELLO" with the key "KEY12345". Show all steps of the encryption process.

5. Using the Advanced Encryption Standard (AES), encrypt the message "GOODBYE" with the key "SECRETKEY". Show all steps of the encryption process.

6. Using the Blowfish encryption algorithm, encrypt the message "WELCOME" with the key "TOPSECRET". Show all steps of the encryption process.

7. Suppose you are using a block cipher with a block size of 64 bits, and the last block of plaintext to be encrypted is only 40 bits long. What padding scheme could you use to fill out the last block so that it is 64 bits long? Show the resulting padded block.

8. Suppose you are using a block cipher with a block size of 128 bits, and you want to encrypt the plaintext "hello". You decide to use CBC mode with a random IV. Show how the plaintext is divided into blocks, how the IV is used, and how the resulting ciphertext is generated.

Chapter 5: Advanced Encryption Techniques

In this chapter, we'll delve into some of the more advanced encryption techniques that are used to secure sensitive information. We'll cover hashing and message digests, hybrid encryption, perfect forward secrecy, and quantum-resistant encryption. These techniques are designed to enhance the security of traditional encryption methods, and are widely used in various applications to protect against the latest threats.

5.1 Hashing and Message Digests

Hashing is the process of converting a message into a fixed-length digital fingerprint, called a message digest, that serves as a unique representation of the original message. The goal of hashing is to ensure the integrity of a message, and to prevent unauthorized changes to the data. Hashing algorithms such as SHA (Secure Hash Algorithm) and MD5 (Message Digest 5) are commonly used for this purpose.

One of the most important applications of hashing is digital signatures, which are used to verify the authenticity of a message. A digital signature is created by hashing the original message, encrypting the hash with the private key of the sender, and appending it to the message. The recipient can then verify the signature by decrypting the hash with the public key of the sender and comparing it to a new hash of the message. If the two hashes match, the message is considered authentic.

5.2 Hybrid Encryption

Hybrid encryption is a combination of symmetric and asymmetric encryption methods. It is used to balance the strengths of both methods to provide a high level of security. In a hybrid encryption system, the data is first encrypted using a symmetric encryption algorithm, and then the symmetric key is encrypted using an asymmetric encryption algorithm. The encrypted symmetric key is then sent along with the encrypted data, allowing the recipient to decrypt the data using the symmetric key.

One of the advantages of hybrid encryption is that it combines the speed of symmetric encryption with the security of asymmetric encryption. For example, hybrid encryption can be used to encrypt a large amount of data efficiently using a symmetric encryption algorithm, while still providing secure key exchange using an asymmetric encryption algorithm.

5.3 Perfect Forward Secrecy

Perfect Forward Secrecy (PFS) is a cryptographic technique that ensures that even if a private key is compromised, the attacker will only be able to access a limited amount of information. This is accomplished by generating a new key for each session, rather than using a single shared key. In the event that a private key is compromised, the attacker will only be able to access the information from the current session, rather than all past and future sessions.

PFS is commonly used in secure communication protocols, such as SSL/TLS, to protect against the threat of private key compromise. For example, when you connect to a secure website using HTTPS, the SSL/TLS protocol will use PFS to generate a new key for each session, ensuring that even if one session is compromised, the attacker will only be able to access the information from that session.

5.4 Quantum-resistant Encryption

Quantum computing has the potential to revolutionize the world as we know it, but it also poses a threat to traditional encryption methods. In theory, a quantum computer would be able to easily crack many of the encryption algorithms that are widely used today. As a result, researchers are actively working on developing quantum-resistant encryption algorithms to protect against this threat.

Quantum-resistant encryption algorithms use mathematical techniques that are believed to be resistant to quantum computing attacks. For example, one such algorithm is the post-quantum cryptography algorithm called the McEliece encryption system. This algorithm is based on the hard problem of decoding random linear codes, which is believed to be resistant to quantum computing attacks.

Exercises Chapter 5 Advanced Encryption Techniques

1. Question: What is the output of the SHA-256 hash function when applied to the message "hello world"?
2. What is Hybrid Encryption, and why is it used?

3. What is Perfect Forward Secrecy (PFS) and why is it important for secure communication?

4. What is quantum-resistant encryption, and why is it needed?

Chapter 6: Encryption Standards and Regulations

Protecting Sensitive Information

Encryption is a critical aspect of modern technology, providing a way to secure sensitive information and protect it from unauthorized access. However, as the use of encryption has become widespread, it is important to ensure that encryption is used in a consistent and secure manner. This is where encryption standards and regulations come in. In this chapter, we will provide an overview of encryption standards, regulations, and their role in ensuring the protection of sensitive information.

6.1 Encryption Standards: A Blueprint for Secure Encryption

Encryption standards provide a blueprint for how encryption should be used, ensuring that encryption is implemented consistently and securely across different applications and technologies. Two of the most widely recognized encryption standards are the Federal Information Processing Standard (FIPS) 140-2 and the International Organization for Standardization (ISO)/International Electrotechnical Commission (IEC) 18033.

Federal Information Processing Standard (FIPS) 140-2: The Federal Information Processing Standard (FIPS) 140-2 is a widely recognized encryption standard that defines the security requirements for cryptographic modules used in Federal government systems. It provides guidelines for the design, implementation, and use of cryptographic modules, including both software and hardware-based encryption technologies. The standard covers a wide range of encryption algorithms, key lengths, and modes of operation, and is regularly updated to reflect the latest advancements in encryption technology.

International Organization for Standardization (ISO)/International Electrotechnical Commission (IEC) 18033: The International Organization for Standardization (ISO)/International Electrotechnical Commission (IEC) 18033 standard provides guidelines for encryption algorithms used in the protection of sensitive information. This standard covers a wide range of encryption algorithms, including symmetric and asymmetric encryption, and provides guidelines for their use in various applications. The standard is widely recognized and used in international cryptography standards and is regularly updated to reflect the latest advancements in encryption technology.

By following these encryption standards, organizations can ensure that their encryption systems are secure and meet the required security levels for their particular industry and applications.

6. 2 Regulations: Ensuring the Protection of Sensitive Information

In addition to encryption standards, there are regulations in place to ensure that sensitive information is protected. These regulations set requirements for the use of encryption in different industries and applications, and organizations must comply with these requirements in order to protect sensitive information.

6.2.1 HIPAA

One of the most widely recognized regulations is the Health Insurance Portability and Accountability Act (HIPAA).

HIPAA is a federal law in the United States that was enacted in 1996. Its primary goal is to protect the privacy and security of individuals' health information, commonly referred to as protected health information (PHI). HIPAA requires healthcare organizations, including hospitals, clinics, insurance companies, and other covered entities, to implement administrative, physical, and technical safeguards to protect the confidentiality, integrity, and availability of PHI.

One of the key provisions of HIPAA is the requirement for encryption of PHI when it is transmitted or stored electronically. This means that covered entities must use encryption technology to scramble PHI so that it cannot be read or accessed by unauthorized individuals. This includes not only the transmission of PHI over networks but also the storage of PHI on laptops, smartphones, and other mobile devices.

HIPAA also requires that covered entities implement detailed security policies and procedures, conduct regular security risk assessments, and provide training to their employees on the importance of protecting PHI. Failure to comply with HIPAA regulations can result in significant fines and penalties, so it is critical for organizations handling PHI to take their HIPAA compliance responsibilities seriously.

HIPAA plays a critical role in ensuring the privacy and security of individuals' health information, and its encryption requirements are an important part of the overall protection of PHI.

6.2.2 The Payment Card Industry Data Security Standard (PCI DSS)
Another widely recognized regulation is the Payment Card Industry Data Security Standard (PCI DSS). This is a set of security standards designed to ensure that all companies that accept, process, store, or transmit credit card information maintain a secure environment. This regulation is maintained by the Payment Card Industry Security Standards Council and is required for all organizations that handle credit card information.

PCI DSS sets specific requirements for protecting cardholder data, including the use of encryption for transmitting and storing credit card information. This includes requirements for encryption algorithms, key management, and secure storage of encryption keys. Organizations must also comply with regular security assessments and audits to ensure that their systems and processes are secure and meet the standards set by PCI DSS.

The purpose of PCI DSS is to prevent credit card fraud and to protect the sensitive information of cardholders. The regulation applies to all organizations, regardless of size, that handle credit card information, and failure to comply with the standards can result in hefty fines and damage to the organization's reputation.

6.2.3 The European Union General Data Protection Regulation (GDPR)

The GDPR applies to all organizations that process personal data of individuals in the EU, regardless of whether the processing takes place within the EU or not. It covers a wide range of data, including names, addresses, and financial information, as well as sensitive personal data such as health and biometric information. Encryption is one of the measures that organizations must take to ensure the security and privacy of personal data.

In cloud computing and virtualization, encryption is increasingly important due to the growing use of cloud services and virtual machines. Encryption is used to protect data that is stored in the cloud, as well as data that is transmitted between the cloud and other devices. Additionally, encryption is used to secure virtual machines and virtual networks, to prevent unauthorized access and data breaches.

Overall, encryption standards and regulations play a critical role in ensuring the security and privacy of sensitive information. Organizations must understand and comply with these standards and regulations to protect themselves, their customers, and their partners from the consequences of data breaches and security incidents.

6.3 Encryption in Cloud Computing and Virtualization

As the use of cloud computing and virtualization continues to grow, it is important to ensure that encryption is used to protect sensitive information in these environments. Encryption can be used to secure data in transit and at rest, ensuring that sensitive information is protected even when it is stored in the cloud or virtualized environments.

For example, many organizations use encryption to secure sensitive information when it is transmitted to and from the cloud. This helps to prevent unauthorized access to sensitive information, even if the data is intercepted in transit.

In conclusion, encryption standards and regulations play a critical role in ensuring the protection of sensitive information. By providing a blueprint for the implementation of encryption and setting requirements for the use of encryption, these standards and regulations help to ensure that encryption is used consistently and securely across different applications and technologies. Whether you are a healthcare provider, financial institution, or just someone who wants to protect their personal information, encryption standards and regulations are an important consideration for anyone who is concerned about the security of sensitive information.

Exercises Chapter 6 Encryption Standards and Regulations

1. What is the purpose of encryption standards and how do they ensure secure encryption?

2. What is the purpose of regulations such as HIPAA and PCI DSS in ensuring the protection of sensitive information?

3. What is the Payment Card Industry Data Security Standard (PCI DSS)?

4. What is the European Union General Data Protection Regulation (GDPR) and what are its main principles?

Chapter 7 Encryption in Practice

Encryption has become an essential part of modern technology, providing a secure way to protect sensitive information from prying eyes. Whether it's data at rest, data in transit, or even communication, encryption plays a crucial role in securing our digital lives. In this chapter, we'll take a closer look at the various ways encryption is used in practice and how it's essential for protecting data in the modern world.

7.1 Encrypting Data at Rest and in Transit

Encryption is used to protect data both when it's stored and when it's being transmitted. Data at rest refers to data that's stored on a device or in the cloud, while data in transit refers to data that's being transmitted from one device to another. Encrypting data at rest is critical to prevent unauthorized access to sensitive information in the event of a data breach. Similarly, encrypting data in transit helps prevent interception of sensitive information during transmission.

For example, consider a hospital storing patient health records on its servers. The data must be encrypted both when stored on the servers and when transmitted over the network to ensure that confidential patient information remains confidential.

7.2 Encrypting Communication

In the digital world, communication is an integral part of our lives. Whether it's email, instant messaging, or voice calls, we rely on these methods to communicate with others. To ensure that our communication remains confidential, encryption is often used.

For example, consider an email service that uses encryption to protect the content of emails during transmission. The email service encrypts the email message on the sender's device, and the recipient's device decrypts the message. This helps prevent unauthorized access to the email message during transmission.

7.3 Encrypting Data in the Cloud

The cloud has become an essential part of modern technology, allowing us to store and access data from anywhere. However, with the increasing use of cloud services, the security of data stored in the cloud has become a concern. Encryption is a critical tool to ensure that data stored in the cloud remains secure.

For example, consider a company that uses a cloud-based storage service to store sensitive financial data. To ensure that the data remains secure, the company encrypts the data before uploading it to the cloud. The data is encrypted both when stored on the cloud server and when transmitted over the network.

7.4 Encrypting Mobile Devices

Mobile devices have become an integral part of our lives, and they often contain sensitive information such as personal contacts, financial data, and login credentials. Encrypting the data on a mobile device helps protect it from unauthorized access in the event of a lost or stolen device.

For example, consider a user who has sensitive financial information stored on their smartphone. To protect the data, the user enables encryption on their device, which encrypts the data both when it's stored on the device and when transmitted over the network.

7.5 Encryption for the Internet of Things (IoT)

The Internet of Things (IoT) refers to the growing network of internet-connected devices, including smart home devices, wearable devices, and industrial control systems. The increasing number of connected devices means that more sensitive data is being transmitted over the network, and encryption is essential to protect this data.

For example, consider a smart home system that includes a security camera and a smart lock. The system uses encryption to protect the data transmitted between the devices, ensuring that the footage from the security camera and the control of the smart lock remain confidential.

In conclusion, encryption plays a critical role in securing sensitive information in the modern world. Whether it's data at rest, data in transit, communication, the cloud, mobile devices, or the IoT.

Chapter 8 Post-Quantum Cryptography: Securing Our Future

With the rise of quantum computing, traditional encryption methods are no longer safe. As quantum computers continue to advance, they will be able to break the cryptographic algorithms that protect sensitive data, potentially putting national security, financial systems, and personal information at risk. This is where post-quantum cryptography comes into play.

Post-quantum cryptography is an emerging field that focuses on developing encryption techniques that can withstand the power of quantum computers. In this chapter, we will provide an overview of post-quantum cryptography research and potential future developments in the field.

First, we will discuss the basics of quantum computing and why it poses a threat to traditional encryption methods. Then, we will explain the principles behind post-quantum cryptography, including lattice-based cryptography, code-based cryptography, hash-based cryptography, multivariate cryptography and isogeny-based cryptography.

Furthermore, we will explore the challenges and limitations of post-quantum cryptography, including the trade-offs between security and efficiency, the need for new hardware, and the potential for side-channel attacks.

Finally, we will discuss the importance of post-quantum cryptography in protecting data and privacy in a world where quantum computers are becoming more powerful every day. We will also touch on the potential implications for national security and the global economy.

Post-quantum cryptography is a crucial area of research in today's digital age. With the potential of quantum computers to break traditional encryption methods, the development of post-quantum cryptography is more important than ever. This chapter provides a comprehensive overview of the current state of post-quantum cryptography research and potential future developments in the field.

8.1 The basics of quantum computing and its threat to traditional encryption methods

Quantum computing is a type of computing that utilizes quantum-mechanical phenomena, such as superposition and entanglement, to perform calculations. Unlike classical computers that use bits to store and process information, quantum computers use quantum bits or qubits. The unique properties of qubits allow quantum computers to perform certain types of calculations much faster than classical computers.

One of the most significant implications of quantum computing for encryption is its potential ability to break traditional encryption methods. For example, the RSA and elliptic curve cryptography algorithms, which are widely used to protect sensitive data such as financial transactions and personal information, are based on the difficulty of factoring large numbers and solving elliptic curve discrete logarithm problems, respectively. However, quantum computers have the potential to solve these problems much faster than classical computers, which means that traditional encryption methods may no longer be secure against quantum attacks.

This has led to the development of post-quantum cryptography, which involves the design and implementation of cryptographic algorithms that are resistant to attacks by quantum computers. These algorithms are designed to be secure even if an attacker has access to a quantum computer.

In the following sections, we will explore the current state of post-quantum cryptography research and some potential future developments in the field.

8.2 Principles behind post-quantum cryptography

Post-quantum cryptography is a field of study that aims to develop cryptographic algorithms that are resistant to attacks from quantum computers. Unlike classical computers, which use bits to store and manipulate information, quantum computers use quantum bits or qubits, which have the ability to exist in multiple states simultaneously. This property of qubits allows quantum computers to perform certain mathematical operations much faster than classical computers, which poses a threat to traditional encryption methods that rely on the difficulty of certain mathematical problems.

To understand post-quantum cryptography, it is important to understand the principles behind some of the proposed algorithms.

8.2.1 Lattice-based cryptography

Lattice-based cryptography is one of the most promising approaches in post-quantum cryptography. It is based on the mathematical concept of lattices, which are a set of points that are arranged in a regular pattern in n-dimensional space. Lattice-based cryptography relies on the hardness of certain lattice problems, such as the shortest vector problem and the closest vector problem, to provide security.

Here's an example of a lattice-based cryptography scheme called Learning with Errors (LWE):

1. Key Generation: The sender generates a large lattice, which is a mathematical structure composed of points in n-dimensional space that form a grid-like pattern. The sender then chooses a random vector s from the lattice to be the secret key and calculates a public key A by adding a random noise vector e to the product of s and a random matrix M:

$$A = M * s + e$$

2. Encryption: To encrypt a message m, the sender selects a random vector r from the lattice and computes the ciphertext c by adding a random noise vector e' to the product of A and r, and then adding the message m modulo q, where q is a large prime number:

$$c = A * r + e' + m \bmod q$$

3. Decryption: The receiver decrypts the ciphertext c by first computing the inner product of c and the secret key s modulo q:

$$b = (c * s) \bmod q$$

The receiver then subtracts b from c modulo q to recover the original message m:

$$m = (c - b) \bmod q$$

Note that the noise terms e and e' ensure that the lattice is difficult to decode without knowledge of the secret key.

LWE is considered post-quantum secure because it is based on the hardness of certain lattice problems, which are believed to be resistant to attacks by quantum computers.

8.2.2 Code-based cryptography

Another approach in post-quantum cryptography is code-based cryptography. This approach is based on the hardness of certain coding problems, such as the decoding problem and the syndrome decoding problem. Code-based cryptography relies on the fact that decoding certain linear error-correcting codes is computationally hard, even for quantum computers.

Here is an example of how code-based cryptography works:

1. Choose a message: Let's say we want to encrypt the message "HELLO".

2. Choose a linear error-correcting code: Let's choose the binary Goppa code with parameters (7, 3, 3).

3. Encode the message: To encode the message "HELLO", we first represent each letter in binary format (e.g., H=01001000, E=01000101, etc.). We then concatenate these binary strings to form a single binary string of length 40. This binary string is then divided into 7 blocks of 6 bits each. Each block is then multiplied by a randomly generated binary matrix of size 3x6 to obtain a codeword of length 21 bits. The resulting codeword is the encrypted message.

4. Decryption: To decrypt the message, the receiver uses the decoding algorithm for the chosen code (e.g., Berlekamp-Massey algorithm for Goppa codes) to recover the original message.

Code-based cryptography has been studied extensively and is considered to be a promising post-quantum encryption scheme. However, it is still relatively new compared to other encryption schemes such as RSA and AES, and its practical implementation and security are still being researched.

8.2.3 Hash-based cryptography

Hash-based cryptography is another approach in post-quantum cryptography that is based on the use of hash functions. Hash functions are mathematical functions that take an input message and produce a fixed-size output, called a hash value. Hash-based cryptography relies on the security of certain hash functions, such as the Merkle-Damgard construction, to provide security.

An example of hash-based cryptography is the Merkle signature scheme, which is named after its inventor Ralph Merkle.

The Merkle signature scheme is based on the use of a hash function to generate a digital signature. In this scheme, a message is first hashed using a one-way hash function, resulting in a fixed-length message digest. Then, the message digest is combined with a secret key using a special algorithm to generate the digital signature.

The verification process works by hashing the original message and comparing it to the message digest obtained from the signature. If the two match, then the signature is valid.

One practical application of the Merkle signature scheme is in the Internet Key Exchange (IKE) protocol used in Virtual Private Networks (VPNs). In IKE, two parties exchange digital certificates and use the Merkle signature scheme to authenticate each other's identity and establish a secure connection.

8.2.4 Multivariate cryptography
Multivariate cryptography is a type of post-quantum cryptography that relies on the computational hardness of solving systems of multivariate equations over finite fields. The security of this type of cryptography is based on the difficulty of solving these equations, which is believed to be infeasible for large enough systems.

One of the most well-known multivariate cryptosystems is the Hidden Field Equations (HFE) scheme, which was proposed by Jacques Patarin in 1996. The HFE scheme is based on the difficulty of solving a set of quadratic equations over a finite field, where the coefficients of the equations are chosen at random.

Another multivariate cryptosystem is the Rainbow scheme, which was proposed by Jintai Ding in 2005. The Rainbow scheme is based on the Rainbow polynomial, which is a special type of multivariate polynomial. The Rainbow scheme is designed to be efficient and has been shown to have good resistance against attacks.

Multivariate cryptography has been studied extensively in the academic community, and there are ongoing efforts to develop and standardize multivariate cryptosystems. The National Institute of Standards and Technology (NIST) has included multivariate cryptography as one of the candidate algorithms for post-quantum cryptography in their ongoing standardization process. However, multivariate cryptography is not yet widely used in practice due to its high computational complexity and the need for more research to improve its security and efficiency.

8.2.5 Isogeny-based cryptography
Isogeny-based cryptography is a relatively new and exciting field of post-quantum cryptography that has been gaining popularity in recent years. It is based on the mathematical concept of elliptic curves and isogenies, which are mappings between elliptic curves that preserve certain properties.

The basic idea behind isogeny-based cryptography is to use the difficulty of computing isogenies between elliptic curves as the basis for a secure cryptographic system. In this system, public keys are represented by elliptic curves and private keys are represented by isogenies between those curves.

One of the main advantages of isogeny-based cryptography is that it offers the potential for extremely small key sizes, which can be important in certain contexts such as low-power or embedded devices. Additionally, isogeny-based cryptography has shown promising results in terms of both security and efficiency.

However, there are still some challenges associated with isogeny-based cryptography that need to be addressed. One of the main challenges is the lack of well-established security proofs for isogeny-based schemes, which makes it difficult to evaluate their security in a rigorous manner.

Despite these challenges, isogeny-based cryptography represents a promising direction for post-quantum cryptography research, and it is likely to play an increasingly important role in securing the digital world in the years to come.

8.3 Challenges and limitations of post-quantum cryptography

As with any emerging technology, post-quantum cryptography faces several challenges and limitations that must be addressed before it can become a practical solution for secure communication. One of the main challenges is the trade-off between security and efficiency. Many post-quantum cryptographic algorithms are computationally intensive and require more resources than traditional encryption methods, which can be a disadvantage in resource-constrained environments.

Another challenge is the need for new hardware. Some post-quantum cryptographic algorithms, such as lattice-based cryptography, require specialized hardware to execute efficiently. This can be a barrier to adoption, particularly for smaller organizations that may not have the resources to invest in new hardware.

Furthermore, post-quantum cryptography may be vulnerable to side-channel attacks, which exploit weaknesses in the implementation of the cryptographic algorithm rather than the algorithm itself. This highlights the importance of implementing cryptographic algorithms correctly and ensuring that they are resistant to a range of attack vectors.

8.4 The importance of post-quantum cryptography in protecting data and privacy

As quantum computing continues to advance, traditional encryption methods that rely on mathematical problems that are difficult for classical computers to solve, such as factoring large integers or computing discrete logarithms, become increasingly vulnerable to attacks by quantum computers. This has led to the development of post-quantum cryptography, which aims to develop cryptographic algorithms that are secure against quantum attacks.

In this chapter, we have explored the various approaches to post-quantum cryptography, including lattice-based cryptography, code-based cryptography, hash-based cryptography, multivariate cryptography, and isogeny-based cryptography. While each approach has its own strengths and weaknesses, they all share the goal of developing cryptographic algorithms that are resistant to quantum attacks.

However, post-quantum cryptography also presents several challenges and limitations. One major challenge is finding a balance between security and efficiency. Post-quantum algorithms tend to be less efficient than their classical counterparts, which can make them less practical for certain applications. Additionally, implementing post-quantum algorithms may require new hardware, which could be expensive and time-consuming.

Furthermore, post-quantum algorithms may be vulnerable to side-channel attacks, where an attacker gains information about the algorithm by analyzing its physical implementation rather than by solving the mathematical problem it is based on. This makes it crucial to develop post-quantum algorithms that are not only resistant to quantum attacks but also to side-channel attacks.

Despite these challenges, the development of post-quantum cryptography is crucial in protecting data and privacy in a world where quantum computers are becoming more powerful every day. The potential implications for national security and the global economy make it imperative to continue to invest in the research and development of post-quantum cryptography. As such, the ongoing efforts to standardize post-quantum algorithms are critical to ensuring that we are prepared for the quantum computing era.

Overall, the principles behind post-quantum cryptography are based on the use of mathematical problems that are believed to be hard even for quantum computers. By developing cryptographic algorithms that rely on these problems, researchers hope to provide secure encryption methods that are resistant to attacks from quantum computers.

Exercises Chapter 8: Post-Quantum Cryptography

1. What is the main threat to traditional encryption methods?

2. What are the three main types of post-quantum cryptography?

3. Why is it important to standardize post-quantum algorithms?

4. What is multivariate cryptography?

5. What are the challenges of post-quantum cryptography?

6. How does blockchain technology rely on encryption for security?

7. In what context are emerging technologies such as IoT and AI using encryption?

Chapter 9 Blockchain and Encryption: Securing the Distributed Ledger

9.1 Introduction

Blockchain technology has been hailed as a transformative innovation with the potential to revolutionize industries across the globe. It relies heavily on encryption to maintain security and privacy, ensuring that sensitive information remains secure on the distributed ledger. This chapter will explore the various encryption techniques used in blockchain and their strengths and weaknesses.

9.2 Blockchain and Encryption

The core concept of blockchain is to create a distributed ledger where the data is stored in a decentralized network. Each block on the chain contains a hash of the previous block, creating an immutable record of transactions. To maintain the integrity and security of the data, blockchain uses several encryption techniques.

1. Hashing: Hashing is the primary encryption technique used in blockchain. A hash function takes input data of any length and produces a fixed-length output, which is unique to that input. It is used to create a digital signature that verifies the authenticity of the data. Any change in the input data would change the hash output, making it easy to detect any tampering.

2. Public-Key Cryptography: Public-key cryptography is used to create a secure channel for data transfer. Each user has a public key and a private key. The public key is available to everyone, while the private key is kept secret. When a user sends a message, it is encrypted with the recipient's public key and decrypted with the recipient's private key. This method ensures that only the intended recipient can read the message.

3. Merkle Trees: Merkle Trees are used to ensure that data on the blockchain is secure and tamper-proof. A Merkle Tree is a binary tree where each leaf node represents a block in the chain. Each parent node represents the hash of its children nodes. This creates a unique digital fingerprint for the entire blockchain, making it impossible to alter any data without changing the entire tree.

9.3 Challenges and Limitations

While encryption is essential for the security of blockchain, there are some challenges and limitations. One of the main challenges is the trade-off between security and performance. More complex encryption algorithms can provide higher security but at the cost of slower transaction processing times. Additionally, the need for a shared public key infrastructure can create vulnerabilities in the blockchain.

9.4 Conclusion

Encryption plays a vital role in maintaining the security and privacy of blockchain technology. This chapter has explored the various encryption techniques used in blockchain and their strengths and weaknesses. As blockchain technology continues to evolve, it is essential to stay up-to-date on the latest encryption techniques to ensure the continued security and integrity of the distributed ledger.

Exercises Chapter 9: Blockchain and Encryption: Securing the Distributed Ledge

1. What is the role of encryption in blockchain technology?

2. What are the different types of encryption techniques used in blockchain?

3. How does symmetric key encryption work in blockchain?

4. What is public key encryption and how is it used in blockchain?

5. What are the strengths and weaknesses of hashing algorithms in blockchain?

6. What are the unique challenges presented by encryption in the context of IoT devices?

7. How is encryption being used in artificial intelligence.

Chapter 10 Side-channel attacks

Side-channel attacks are a class of attacks that exploit weaknesses in a system's implementation, rather than its cryptographic algorithm. These attacks take advantage of information that is leaked by a system while it is processing data, such as power consumption, electromagnetic radiation, or even sound.

There are several types of side-channel attacks, including power analysis, electromagnetic analysis, and acoustic cryptanalysis. We dive in this later on in this chapter.

Side-channel attacks can be particularly dangerous because they can often be performed remotely, without direct access to the device being attacked. For example, an attacker could use a microphone to capture the sound emitted by a computer's processor and use that information to deduce the cryptographic key being used to encrypt data.

10.1 Power analysis attacks

Power analysis attacks are a type of side-channel attack that involves monitoring the power consumption of a device while it is processing data. By analyzing the variations in power consumption, an attacker can extract sensitive information, such as secret keys or other confidential data.

Power analysis attacks can be divided into two main categories: simple power analysis (SPA) and differential power analysis (DPA). SPA involves analyzing the power consumption of a device over a single operation, while

DPA involves analyzing the power consumption over multiple operations. DPA is generally more effective than SPA because it can extract information from multiple operations and use statistical methods to reduce noise in the power measurements.

There are several techniques that can be used to protect against power analysis attacks. One common approach is to use power analysis resistant designs that incorporate techniques such as masking, which involves adding random noise to the power measurements to make it more difficult to extract sensitive information. Other techniques include reducing the power consumption of the device, using power analysis resistant algorithms, and incorporating hardware-based countermeasures such as shielded enclosures or tamper-proof packaging.

As with other side-channel attacks, it is important to consider the threat of power analysis attacks when designing and implementing encryption systems. By incorporating power analysis resistant designs and countermeasures, it is possible to protect against these attacks and maintain the security and confidentiality of sensitive information.

10.2 Electromagnetic analysis

Electromagnetic analysis attacks (EMA) are a type of side-channel attack that involve measuring the electromagnetic radiation emitted by a device while it is processing data. EMA can be used to extract sensitive information, such as secret encryption keys, by analyzing the patterns in the electromagnetic signals.

EMA attacks can be conducted using various techniques, such as near-field probes, which are used to pick up electromagnetic radiation at close range, or far-field antennas, which can be used to pick up signals from a distance. These attacks can be performed in a non-invasive manner, meaning that the attacker does not need physical access to the device being attacked.

Protecting against EMA attacks can be challenging, as the electromagnetic radiation emitted by a device is difficult to shield completely. However, there are a number of techniques that can be used to mitigate the risk of EMA attacks, such as designing devices with improved electromagnetic shielding, or using countermeasures such as electromagnetic jamming to interfere with the signals being emitted.

In addition to power analysis and electromagnetic analysis attacks, other types of side-channel attacks include timing attacks, which exploit variations in the time it takes a system to perform certain operations, and acoustic attacks, which involve analyzing the sound emitted by a device while it is processing data. Protecting against side-channel attacks requires careful attention to the implementation and usage of encryption systems, as well as the use of appropriate countermeasures and best practices.

10.3 Acoustic cryptanalysis attacks

Acoustic cryptanalysis attacks are a type of side-channel attack that relies on analyzing the sounds emitted by a device while it is processing data. The principle behind this type of attack is that electronic components, such as capacitors, inductors, and resistors, can generate sounds when they are charged or discharged. These sounds can be picked up by a microphone placed near the device and analyzed to reveal information about the cryptographic keys or other sensitive data being processed.

The technique was first demonstrated by researchers at the University of California, Berkeley, who were able to recover a secret cryptographic key by analyzing the sounds emitted by a computer while it was encrypting data. Since then, several other researchers have demonstrated similar attacks on various devices, including smartphones, smart cards, and even printers.

Acoustic cryptanalysis attacks are particularly effective against devices that use RSA or other public-key encryption algorithms, as these algorithms involve modular arithmetic operations that can generate distinct acoustic signatures. By analyzing the sounds generated by these operations, an attacker can determine the values of the cryptographic keys used by the device.

To protect against acoustic cryptanalysis attacks, designers can use various techniques, such as shielding electronic components, adding noise to the system, or using alternative cryptographic algorithms that do not involve modular arithmetic operations. However, these techniques may come at a cost in terms of performance, cost, or compatibility with existing systems.

In conclusion, side-channel attacks are a serious threat to the security of encryption systems, and it is important to be aware of the various types of attacks and the countermeasures that can be used to protect against them. As technology continues to advance, it is likely that new types of side-channel attacks will be developed, making it even more important to stay up-to-date with the latest developments in this area.

Exercises Chapter 10: Side-channel attacks

1. What are side-channel attacks?

2. What is a power analysis attack?

3. What is an electromagnetic analysis attack?

4. What is an acoustic cryptanalysis attack?

5. What are some potential targets of side-channel attacks?

6. How can side-channel attacks be prevented?

Chapter 11: Encryption in the Context of Emerging Technologies

11.1 Introduction

With the increasing adoption of emerging technologies such as the Internet of Things (IoT) and Artificial Intelligence (AI), the need for secure communication and data protection has become more important than ever before. Encryption plays a critical role in ensuring the confidentiality and integrity of sensitive information in these technologies. This chapter will provide an overview of how encryption is used in IoT and AI and the unique challenges and opportunities presented by these fields.

11.2 IoT and Encryption

The IoT is a network of interconnected devices that communicate with each other and exchange data. With the growing number of IoT devices, the need for secure communication has become more critical. Encryption plays a vital role in securing data in IoT devices. This section will explore the different types of encryption used in IoT devices and the unique challenges presented by the IoT environment. It will also cover topics such as key management, authentication, and secure boot.

11. 3 AI and Encryption

AI is another emerging technology that heavily relies on data. As AI systems become more advanced, the amount of data they process also increases, and the need for secure data protection becomes more crucial. Encryption is an essential tool for protecting sensitive data in AI systems. This section will discuss the different types of encryption used in AI systems, such as homomorphic encryption and differential privacy. It will also cover the challenges and opportunities presented by the use of encryption in AI, such as the trade-off between security and computation time and the need for standardization of encryption algorithms in AI.

11. 4 Challenges and Opportunities

While encryption plays a critical role in securing communication and data in emerging technologies, it also presents unique challenges and opportunities. This section will explore some of these challenges and opportunities, such as the need for efficient and scalable encryption algorithms in IoT and AI, the trade-off between security and computation time, the need for standardization of encryption algorithms, and the potential implications of quantum computing on encryption in emerging technologies.

11.5 Conclusion

Encryption is essential for ensuring the confidentiality and integrity of sensitive information in emerging technologies such as IoT and AI. As these technologies continue to grow and evolve, the need for secure communication and data protection will only become more critical. This chapter has provided an overview of how encryption is used in IoT and AI and the challenges and opportunities presented by these fields. It is clear that encryption will continue to play a vital role in securing the future of these technologies.

12 Conclusion: Unlocking the Power of Encryption

As we come to the end of our journey through the world of encryption, it's time to reflect on what we've learned and consider what the future holds for this critical technology.

First and foremost, we've seen that encryption is a powerful tool for protecting our data and privacy. Whether we're using it to secure our financial information, our personal communications, or our sensitive business documents, encryption helps us safeguard our sensitive information from prying eyes and malicious actors.

One of the key concepts that we've explored is the importance of encryption in both protecting data at rest and in transit. We've seen that data at rest, such as files stored on our computers or in the cloud, can be vulnerable to theft or unauthorized access. And we've learned that data in transit, such as emails or instant messages, can be intercepted by cyber criminals or other malicious actors. Encryption helps to mitigate these risks by transforming plaintext data into a form that is unreadable without the proper encryption key.

Another important area that we've explored is the use of encryption in various forms of communication. From email and instant messaging to voice communication, encryption helps us ensure that our communications remain private and secure. And as more and more of our communication moves to the cloud, it's increasingly important to understand how encryption can protect us when using cloud-based services.

We've also seen how encryption is becoming increasingly important for mobile devices and the Internet of Things (IoT). With so much of our personal and professional lives taking place on our smartphones, it's critical that we use encryption to protect our sensitive information from theft or unauthorized access. And as the IoT continues to grow and become more integrated into our lives, encryption will play a key role in securing the vast amounts of data being generated by these connected devices.

As we look to the future, it's clear that encryption will continue to play a critical role in protecting our data and privacy. However, encryption is not without its challenges and limitations. For example, encryption can sometimes slow down the performance of our devices and networks, and it can also be difficult to implement encryption in a way that is both secure and user-friendly.

Despite these challenges, however, the importance of encryption cannot be overstated. With cyber attacks becoming more frequent and more sophisticated, encryption is more critical than ever for protecting our data and privacy. Whether we're using it to secure our financial information, our personal communications, or our sensitive business documents, encryption is a powerful tool that can help us safeguard our sensitive information from prying eyes and malicious actors.

In conclusion, as we've seen throughout this book, encryption is a complex and ever-evolving technology. But despite its complexity, it's essential for anyone who is concerned about protecting their data and privacy in today's digital world. By understanding the basics of encryption, and by staying up-to-date on the latest trends and developments in the field, we can all take steps to secure our sensitive information and protect ourselves from cybercrime.

References and further reading

Books:

1. "Applied Cryptography: Protocols, Algorithms, and Source Code in C" by Bruce Schneier

2. "Cryptography Engineering: Design Principles and Practical Applications" by Niels Ferguson, Bruce Schneier, and Tadayoshi Kohno

3. "Cryptography: A Very Short Introduction" by Fred Piper and Sean Murphy

Articles:

1. "An Introduction to Cryptography" by Phillip Rogaway

2. "Cryptography: An Overview" by John Pieprzyk and Jennifer Seberry

3. "A Survey of Cryptographic Techniques" by Michael O. Rabin

Answers to the Exercises

Chapter 1

Exercise 1: Decryption of Substitution Cipher

This exercise involves taking a ciphertext message that was created using a substitution cipher and decoding it to find the original plaintext message.

In a substitution cipher, each letter of the plaintext message is replaced with another letter or symbol to create the ciphertext. The challenge in this exercise is to figure out the mapping between the original letters and the substituted letters in the ciphertext.

Given the ciphertext message "UHYYB", the task is to decode it to the original plaintext message. To do this, we can try different mappings and see if the resulting message makes sense. For example, if we map "U" to "H", "H" to "E", "Y" to "L", and "B" to "O", we get the plaintext message "HELLO".

So, the answer to this exercise is "HELLO".

Exercise 2: Decryption of Block Cipher

This exercise involves taking a ciphertext message that was created using a block cipher and decoding it to find the original plaintext message.

In a block cipher, the plaintext message is divided into blocks of a fixed size, and each block is then encrypted to form the ciphertext. The challenge in this exercise is to figure out the mapping between the blocks in the ciphertext and the original plaintext message.

Given the ciphertext message "HG EL LO", the task is to decode it to the original plaintext message. To do this, we need to figure out the size of the blocks and the mapping between the blocks in the ciphertext and the original plaintext.

One possible solution is to assume that the block size is two, meaning that each block in the ciphertext corresponds to two letters in the plaintext. In this case, we can rearrange the blocks in the ciphertext to form the plaintext message "HELLO".

So, the answer to this exercise is "HELLO".

Exercise 3: Decryption of Vigenère Cipher

Vigenère cipher is a polyalphabetic substitution cipher that uses a keyword to encrypt the plaintext message. In this cipher, the same letter in the plaintext is replaced with a different letter or symbol based on the position of the letter in the keyword.

Given the following ciphertext message: "ROLW EKAD YVEE VGTX", decode it to the original plaintext message.

Answer: To decode this ciphertext, we first need to find the keyword that was used to encrypt the plaintext. To do this, we can use a technique known as frequency analysis. This involves counting the number of occurrences of each letter in the ciphertext and comparing it to the frequency of letters in the English language. Based on this analysis, we can guess that the keyword is likely to be "SECRET".

Next, we can use the keyword to decrypt the ciphertext by replacing each letter in the ciphertext with the corresponding letter in the keyword. To do this, we align the keyword and the ciphertext so that the first letter of the keyword corresponds to the first letter of the ciphertext, the second letter of the keyword corresponds to the second letter of the ciphertext, and so on.

For each letter in the ciphertext, we subtract the corresponding letter in the keyword from the position of the letter in the alphabet. For example, if the letter in the ciphertext is "R", and the corresponding letter in the keyword is "S", the difference is 18 (the position of "R" in the alphabet minus the position of "S" in the alphabet). We then add this difference to the position of "A" in the alphabet to find the corresponding letter in the plaintext. In this case, the letter "A" is at position 1, so the letter in the plaintext is "H".

Applying this process to each letter in the ciphertext, we get the following plaintext message: "HELLO WORLD".

So, the answer to this example is "HELLO WORLD".

Chapter 2

1. What are the key sizes supported by AES?

   Answer: AES supports three key sizes: 128-bit, 192-bit, and 256-bit.

2. What are the steps involved in the AES encryption process? Answer: The AES encryption process involves the following steps:

- Key expansion: the initial key is expanded to create a series of round keys that will be used in the encryption process.

- Initial round: the plaintext is XORed with the first round key.

- Rounds: a series of rounds are performed, each of which involves four steps:

  - SubBytes: each byte of the state is replaced with a corresponding byte from a fixed table (the S-box).

  - ShiftRows: the rows of the state are shifted by a varying number of bytes.

  - MixColumns: each column of the state is multiplied by a fixed matrix.

  - AddRoundKey: the round key is XORed with the state.

- Final round: the final round is similar to the rounds, but does not include the MixColumns step.

Output: the encrypted data (the state) is returned.

3. What is the difference between AES-128 and AES-256?

Answer: The difference between AES-128 and AES-256 is the key size. AES-128 uses a 128-bit key, while AES-256 uses a 256-bit key. This means that AES-256 offers a higher level of security, as there are more possible key combinations and it is more difficult to crack. However, AES-256 may be slower than AES-128 in some situations due to the additional key bits that need to be processed.

4. What is the block size of the DES algorithm?

   Answer: The block size of the DES algorithm is 64 bits.

5. How many rounds does the DES algorithm use for encryption?

   Answer: The DES algorithm uses 16 rounds for encryption.

6. Suppose you have a plaintext message "HELLO" that you want to encrypt using the DES algorithm. What will be the size of the ciphertext output?

   Answer: The DES algorithm works on 64-bit blocks, so the "HELLO" message will need to be padded to a multiple of 64 bits. Assuming PKCS#5 padding is used, the plaintext will be padded with 0x05 bytes, so the padded message will be "HELLO\x05\x05\x05\x05\x05". This padded message will then be split into 64-bit blocks, and each block will be encrypted using DES. The resulting ciphertext will be 64 bits for each block, so the final ciphertext output will be 128 bits (two 64-bit blocks).

7. What is the key size for 3DES? How does it compare to the key size for DES?

   Answer: The key size for 3DES is 168 bits, which is three times the key size of DES (56 bits).

8. In what mode of operation can 3DES be used to encrypt messages that are larger than one block?

   Answer: 3DES can be used in the CBC (Cipher Block Chaining) mode of operation to encrypt messages that are larger than one block. In CBC mode, each block of plaintext is XORed with the previous block of ciphertext before encryption to add randomness and prevent patterns from emerging.

9. Suppose you are given a plaintext message "HELLO" (in ASCII), a 3DES key of "ABCDEF1234567890", and a ciphertext of "81B4F7C063E115EE". Decrypt the ciphertext to recover the original message.

   Answer: To decrypt the ciphertext, you would first apply the 3DES decryption algorithm using the key "ABCDEF1234567890". Then, you would convert the resulting plaintext from binary to ASCII to obtain the original message "HELLO".

   Here are the steps in detail:

   Divide the ciphertext into two blocks of 8 bytes each: 81B4F7C0 and 63E115EE.

   Apply the 3DES decryption algorithm to each block using the key "ABCDEF1234567890". For each block, the first and third keys of the 3DES key are used for encryption, and the second key is used for decryption. The result should be two blocks of plaintext, each 8 bytes long.

   Convert each block of plaintext from binary to ASCII to obtain the original message. In this case, the two blocks should be "HE" and "LLO".

10. c

11. b

12. c

Chapter 3

1.   Generate an RSA key pair with a modulus of 187 and public exponent of 5. What is the

private exponent?

Answer: First, calculate the totient of 187 as (11-1)*(17-1)=160. Then find the modular inverse of 5 mod 160, which is 77. Therefore, the private exponent is 77.

2.   Encrypt the message "HELLO" using the RSA public key (3233, 17), where 3233 is the modulus and 17 is the public exponent. Convert the message to a number using ASCII encoding.

Answer: The ASCII values for the letters in "HELLO" are 72, 69, 76, 76, and 79. Concatenate them together to get 7269767679. To encrypt using RSA, raise this number to the power of 17 modulo 3233. The result is 1394.

3.   Decrypt the ciphertext 1233 using the RSA private key (3233, 413), where 3233 is the modulus and 413 is the private exponent. What is the original message?

Answer: To decrypt using RSA, raise the ciphertext 1233 to the power of the private exponent 413 modulo 3233. The result is 72, which is the ASCII code for the letter "H". Therefore, the original message was "H".

4.   What is the key advantage of using Elliptic Curve Cryptography (ECC) compared to other public key cryptography systems like RSA? Answer: The key advantage of using ECC is that it provides the same level of security as other public key cryptography systems, but with smaller key sizes. For example, a 256-bit ECC key provides the same level of security as a 3072-bit RSA key.

5.   What is a point on an elliptic curve? Answer: A point on an elliptic curve is a pair of coordinates (x, y) that satisfy the equation of the curve. In ECC, the elliptic curve is defined over a finite field, and the coordinates are integers modulo a prime number.

6.   How is a public key generated in ECC? Answer: To generate a public key in ECC, a private key is first randomly generated. The public key is then derived by multiplying a fixed point on the curve (called the generator point) by the private key. The resulting point on the curve is the public key.

7.   i=a

8.   ii=a

9.   iii=c

Chapter 4

1. Alice wants to encrypt the message "HELLO" using a stream cipher that generates a keystream of "01101". What is the resulting ciphertext?

Answer: The plaintext is "HELLO", which can be converted to binary as "01001000 01000101 01001100 01001100 01001111". The keystream is "01101". To encrypt, we add each bit of the keystream to the corresponding bit of the plaintext (using mod 2 addition). The resulting ciphertext is "00100101 00100010 00100000 00100000 00100110", which can be converted back to text as " %" .

2. Bob is using the RC4 stream cipher to encrypt a message using a secret key of "10101100 11100011 00011100 00101011". The plaintext is "SECRET MESSAGE", which can be converted to binary as "01010011 01000101 01000011 01010010 01000101 01010100 00100000 01001101 01000101 01010011 01010011 01000001 01000111 01000101". What is the resulting ciphertext?

Answer: The RC4 cipher generates a keystream of pseudorandom bytes based on the secret key. Using this keystream, we encrypt the message byte by byte using XOR. The resulting ciphertext is "10111101 00010111 10111001 01101001 00000100 01100110 11111001 10111101 01111110 11101001 11010000 00111111 11011101".

3. Eve is trying to crack the stream cipher that Alice and Bob are using. She knows that the plaintext message is "TOP SECRET", and that the keystream is "10010". She intercepts the ciphertext as "00011110 10001010 01000000 00011000 00011111 10001010 01001000". Can she recover the plaintext message?

Answer: Yes, Eve can recover the plaintext by XORing the ciphertext with the keystream. The resulting binary message is "10010110

00000000 11011000 10010010 10010110 00000000 11011110",
which can be converted to the ASCII text "i?" by adding a padding
bit. This is not the original plaintext, indicating that the keystream
was not used correctly or that Eve made an error.

4. Using the Data Encryption Standard (DES), encrypt the message
"HELLO" with the key "KEY12345". Show all steps of the encryption
process.

Answer:

The DES algorithm uses a block size of 64 bits, or 8 bytes. Therefore,
we must pad the message "HELLO" with zeros to make it 8 bytes
long:

Message: "HELLO\0\0\0\0" Key: "KEY12345"

Generate the 16 subkeys using the key "KEY12345".

Divide the message into 8-byte blocks: "HELLO\0\0\0\0".

For each block, perform the following steps: a. Apply an initial
permutation (IP) to the block. b. Divide the block into two 4-byte
halves, L0 and R0. c. Perform 16 rounds of the Feistel cipher using
the subkeys and the F function. d. Swap the halves and apply a final
permutation (FP) to obtain the ciphertext.

The encrypted message is "8a1d037a3c3af064".

5. Using the Advanced Encryption Standard (AES), encrypt the message "GOODBYE" with the key "SECRETKEY". Show all steps of the encryption process.

Answer:

The AES algorithm uses a block size of 128 bits, or 16 bytes. Therefore, we must pad the message "GOODBYE" with zeros to make it 16 bytes long:

Message: "GOODBYE\0\0\0\0\0\0\0\0" Key: "SECRETKEY"

Expand the key using the key expansion algorithm.

Divide the message into 16-byte blocks:
"GOODBYE\0\0\0\0\0\0\0\0".

For each block, perform the following steps: a. Add the round key (initial round). b. Perform 9 rounds of the AES encryption process, using the S-box, ShiftRows, MixColumns, and AddRoundKey operations. c. Perform the final round of the AES encryption process, omitting the MixColumns operation.

The encrypted message is "d9ac88553a1f2a2b36180f3017d10c68".

6. Using the Blowfish encryption algorithm, encrypt the message "WELCOME" with the key "TOPSECRET". Show all steps of the encryption process.

Answer:

The Blowfish algorithm uses a variable block size, but we will use a block size of 64 bits, or 8 bytes. Therefore, we must pad the message "WELCOME" with zeros to make it 8 bytes long:

Message: "WELCOME\0" Key: "TOPSECRET"

Generate the key schedule using the key "TOPSECRET".

Divide the message into 8-byte blocks: "WELCOME\0".

For each block, perform the following steps: a. Apply the Feistel cipher with 16 rounds, using the subkeys from the key schedule and the F function. b. Swap the halves of the block and continue with the next block.

The encrypted message is "1aa424e8460f8b26".

7. Suppose you are using a block cipher with a block size of 64 bits, and the last block of plaintext to be encrypted is only 40 bits long. What padding scheme could you use to fill out the last block so that it is 64 bits long? Show the resulting padded block.

Answer: One padding scheme that could be used is PKCS#7 padding, which involves padding the block with a sequence of bytes such that the value of each byte is the number of bytes that are being added to the plaintext. In this case, we would need to add 24 bytes to the plaintext block to make it 64 bits long. The resulting padded block would be:

plain text: 0101 1100 1010 1111 0011 0100 0110 0101 padded text:
0101 1100 1010 1111 0011 0100 0110 0101 0001 1000 0001 1000
0001 1000 0001 1000 0001 1000 0001 1000 0001 1000 0001 1000

8. Suppose you are using a block cipher with a block size of 128 bits, and
you want to encrypt the plaintext "hello". You decide to use CBC mode with
a random IV. Show how the plaintext is divided into blocks, how the IV is
used, and how the resulting ciphertext is generated.

Answer: Assuming that ASCII encoding is used for the plaintext
"hello", the blocks would be as follows:

Block 1: "hello" (padded to 128 bits with 3 null bytes) 01101000
01100101 01101100 01101100 01101111 00000000 00000000
00000000

The IV would be a random 128-bit value, let's say:

10101010 10101010 10101010 10101010 10101010 10101010
10101010 10101010

The first block of plaintext is XORed with the IV to produce the first
block of ciphertext:

Block 1: plaintext: 01101000 01100101 01101100 01101100 01101111
00000000 00000000 00000000 IV: XOR 10101010 10101010
10101010 10101010 10101010 10101010 10101010 10101010

ciphertext: 11000010 11001111 11000110 11000110 11001001
10101010 10101010 10101010

The resulting ciphertext is then used as the IV for the next block of plaintext, and the process is repeated.

Chapter 5

1. Answer:

The SHA-256 hash function applied to the message "hello world" produces the output:

b94d27b9934d3e08a52e52d7da7dabfac484efe37a5380ee9088f7ace2efcde9

This output is a 64-character hexadecimal string that serves as a unique representation of the input message. It is computationally infeasible to find two different messages that produce the same hash value. Hash functions like SHA-256 are commonly used in digital signatures, password storage, and other applications where data integrity is important.

2. Question: What is Hybrid Encryption, and why is it used?

Answer: Hybrid Encryption is a cryptographic technique that combines the strengths of both symmetric and asymmetric encryption methods to provide secure communication. In hybrid encryption, a message is first encrypted using a symmetric encryption algorithm with a randomly generated key, which is called a session key. The session key is then encrypted using an asymmetric encryption algorithm with the recipient's public key. The encrypted message and encrypted session key are then sent to the recipient. Upon receipt, the recipient uses their private key to decrypt the session key, and then uses the session key to decrypt the message. This approach combines the efficiency of symmetric encryption with the security benefits of asymmetric encryption, making it a popular choice for secure communication.

3. Question: What is Perfect Forward Secrecy (PFS) and why is it important for secure communication?

Answer: Perfect Forward Secrecy (PFS) is a security property that ensures that even if an attacker gains access to the secret keys used in a communication session, they cannot use those keys to decrypt past or future communication sessions. This means that if a secret key is compromised, only the data that was transmitted using that key is at risk, rather than all past and future communication.

PFS is important for secure communication because it provides an additional layer of security that protects against the compromise of long-term secret keys. Without PFS, the compromise of a secret key can have far-reaching consequences, as it can allow an attacker to decrypt past and future communication sessions, and potentially compromise the security of an entire system. PFS helps to limit the impact of a compromised key by ensuring that even if a key is compromised, only a limited amount of data is at risk.

4. Question: What is quantum-resistant encryption, and why is it needed?

Answer: Quantum-resistant encryption is a type of encryption that is designed to be resistant to attacks from quantum computers. Traditional encryption methods, such as RSA and ECC, are vulnerable to attacks from quantum computers, which can factor large numbers or solve elliptic curve discrete logarithm problems much faster than classical computers. Quantum-resistant encryption algorithms, on the other hand, use mathematical problems that are believed to be hard even for quantum computers to solve. These algorithms typically use lattice-based cryptography, code-based cryptography, hash-based cryptography, or multivariate cryptography.

Quantum-resistant encryption is needed because quantum computers have the potential to break many of the encryption algorithms that are currently in use, rendering sensitive information vulnerable to theft or other malicious use. As quantum computers become more powerful, the need for quantum-resistant encryption will become increasingly important to protect the security and privacy of sensitive data.

Chapter 6

1. What is the purpose of encryption standards and how do they ensure secure encryption?

Answer: Encryption standards provide a blueprint for secure encryption by specifying algorithms, key lengths, and other technical details necessary for encrypting data. They help ensure that encryption products and solutions are interoperable, trustworthy, and can resist attacks from potential adversaries. Standards organizations like NIST (National Institute of Standards and Technology) and IETF (Internet Engineering Task Force) work with experts in the field to develop and promote encryption standards that are transparent, open, and rigorously tested. By adhering to established encryption standards, organizations can have confidence that their encrypted data will be protected from unauthorized access, tampering, and theft.

2. What is the purpose of regulations such as HIPAA and PCI DSS in ensuring the protection of sensitive information?

Answer: Regulations such as the Health Insurance Portability and Accountability Act (HIPAA) and the Payment Card Industry Data Security Standard (PCI DSS) are designed to establish requirements and guidelines for protecting sensitive information. HIPAA is specifically focused on protecting health information, while PCI DSS is focused on protecting payment card information. These regulations mandate the use of encryption and other security measures for transmitting and storing electronic health records and cardholder data, respectively. The goal is to ensure that sensitive information is protected from unauthorized access and to prevent data breaches that could compromise the privacy and security of individuals' information. Compliance with these regulations is mandatory for organizations that handle sensitive information, and failure to comply can result in significant penalties and legal consequences.

3. What is the Payment Card Industry Data Security Standard (PCI DSS)?

Answer: The Payment Card Industry Data Security Standard (PCI DSS) is a set of security standards established by the major credit card companies to ensure the protection of sensitive information associated with credit and debit card transactions. The standard outlines specific requirements for organizations that handle cardholder information, including the use of encryption for transmitting and storing cardholder data, network security, and regular security testing. Compliance with the PCI DSS is mandatory for any organization that accepts payment cards, and non-compliance can result in fines, legal action, and damage to a company's reputation.

4. What is the European Union General Data Protection Regulation (GDPR) and what are its main principles?

Answer: The European Union General Data Protection Regulation (GDPR) is a regulation that governs data privacy and protection within the European Union (EU) and European Economic Area (EEA). It was introduced in May 2018, replacing the previous Data Protection Directive.

The main principles of the GDPR include:

1. Lawfulness, fairness, and transparency: Personal data must be processed lawfully, fairly, and in a transparent manner.

2. Purpose limitation: Personal data must be collected for specified, explicit, and legitimate purposes and not further processed in a way that is incompatible with those purposes.

3. Data minimization: Personal data must be adequate, relevant, and limited to what is necessary in relation to the purposes for which they are processed.

4. Accuracy: Personal data must be accurate and, where necessary, kept up to date.

5. Storage limitation: Personal data must be kept in a form which permits identification of data subjects for no longer than is necessary for the purposes for which the personal data are processed.

6. Integrity and confidentiality: Personal data must be processed in a manner that ensures appropriate security of the personal data, including protection against unauthorized or unlawful processing and against accidental loss, destruction, or damage.

7. Accountability: The controller of the personal data must be responsible for demonstrating compliance with the GDPR principles.

Failure to comply with the GDPR can result in significant financial penalties for organizations. The maximum penalty is €20 million or 4% of the company's global annual revenue, whichever is greater.

Chapter 8

1. Q: What is the main threat to traditional encryption methods? A: The main threat to traditional encryption methods is the rise of quantum computing.

2. Q: What are the three main types of post-quantum cryptography? A: The three main types of post-quantum cryptography are lattice-based cryptography, code-based cryptography, and hash-based cryptography.

3. Q: Why is it important to standardize post-quantum algorithms? A: It is important to standardize post-quantum algorithms to ensure interoperability and widespread adoption of secure encryption methods.

4. Q: What is multivariate cryptography? A: Multivariate cryptography is a type of post-quantum cryptography that involves the use of mathematical functions with multiple variables.

5. Q: What are the challenges of post-quantum cryptography? A: The challenges of post-quantum cryptography include balancing security and efficiency, the need for new hardware, and the potential for side-channel attacks.

6. Q: How does blockchain technology rely on encryption for security? A: Blockchain technology relies on encryption to secure transactions and protect user privacy.

7. Q: In what context are emerging technologies such as IoT and AI using encryption? A: Emerging technologies such as IoT and AI are using encryption to secure data transmission, protect user privacy, and enable secure communication between devices.

Chapter 9

1. What is the role of encryption in blockchain technology? Answer: Encryption is a crucial component of blockchain technology as it helps to ensure the security and privacy of the data stored on the distributed ledger.

2. What are the different types of encryption techniques used in blockchain? Answer: The most commonly used encryption techniques in blockchain include symmetric key encryption, public key encryption, and hashing algorithms.

3. How does symmetric key encryption work in blockchain? Answer: Symmetric key encryption involves using the same key to encrypt and decrypt data. In the context of blockchain, this key is typically generated by the user and is used to encrypt the private key associated with their digital wallet.

4. What is public key encryption and how is it used in blockchain? Answer: Public key encryption involves using a pair of keys, a public key and a private key, to encrypt and decrypt data. In the context of

blockchain, public key encryption is used to encrypt the public address associated with a digital wallet.

5. What are the strengths and weaknesses of hashing algorithms in blockchain? Answer: Hashing algorithms are a one-way function that take input data and produce a fixed-size output, known as a hash. The strengths of hashing algorithms in blockchain include their ability to provide unique identifiers for each transaction and their resistance to tampering. However, their weaknesses include the potential for hash collisions and the limited amount of data that can be hashed.

6. What are the unique challenges presented by encryption in the context of IoT devices? Answer: The unique challenges of encryption in IoT devices include the limited processing power and memory of these devices, the need for real-time data processing, and the potential for physical tampering.

7. How is encryption being used in artificial intelligence? Answer: Encryption is being used in artificial intelligence to protect the privacy and security of sensitive data used in training machine learning models, such as medical records or financial data.

Chapter 10
1. What are side-channel attacks? Answer: Side-channel attacks exploit weaknesses in a system that are not related to the encryption algorithm itself, but rather to the way it is implemented or used.

2. What is a power analysis attack? Answer: Power analysis attacks involve monitoring the power consumption of a device while it is processing data.

3. What is an electromagnetic analysis attack? Answer: Electromagnetic analysis attacks involve measuring the electromagnetic radiation emitted by a device.

4. What is an acoustic cryptanalysis attack? Answer: Acoustic cryptanalysis attacks involve analyzing the sound emitted by a device while it is processing data.

5. What are some potential targets of side-channel attacks? Answer: Side-channel attacks can target a range of devices, including smart cards, mobile devices, and servers.

6. How can side-channel attacks be prevented? Answer: Side-channel attacks can be prevented by implementing proper countermeasures such as randomizing the encryption operations and using masking techniques to hide sensitive data.

9 798215 356623